The Road

This booklet is like a road map. It will guide you on your journey as you learn to become a servant in the Kingdom of God. You will learn where you are in your walk with the Lord and what steps you can take to grow into spiritual maturity.

There are no right or wrong answers to the questions in this booklet. They are designed to help you see what further preparation you need in order to become an effective minister. Be honest with yourself as you answer these questions. Determining where you need to go requires a clear understanding of where you stand today.

Don't be afraid to evaluate your past Christian growth as you work through the material. Answer each question without worrying about whether or not it might put you in a "bad light" in someone's eyes. The person reviewing your responses with you will be fully committed to helping you grow in Christ, not to belittling or judging you.

Thoughtfully review each page by yourself. Be sure to use a pen as you evaluate your present spiritual condition. Don't ponder the response you should give to the questions! Read and answer them quickly, putting down your first impressions.

After you have finished this guide, your cell leader will arrange a meeting with you to discuss insights about yourself — things you discover as you complete the materials. During this private time of sharing, he or she will offer recommendations to help you develop a fruitful and abundant Christian life.

Together, you and your cell leader will create a Journey Map for equipping. As you complete that journey a year or so from now, you will be amazed at the growth you will have experienced. Your life will be forever changed as a result of developing your walk with the Lord.

Are you ready? Let us begin...

About Your Past . . .

Check [✓] each statement that is true for you:

HOW LONG HAVE YOU BEEN A CHRISTIAN?
☐ Less than three months.　☐ Less than one year.
☐ Less than six months.　☐ Less than two years.
☐ Other: _____

PREVIOUS EXPOSURE TO CHRISTIANITY:
☐ None.
☐ Attended a Christian school.
☐ Previously attended church, but did not believe.
☐ Have never found a church I felt comfortable with.
☐ Have fallen away from following the Lord.
☐ Faithfully participated in the life of a church.
☐ Other: _____

THE FOLLOWING MEMBERS OF YOUR FAMILY ARE CHRISTIANS:
☐ None. I am the first one.
☐ My Mother.
☐ My Father.
☐ Brother(s) or sister(s): _____
☐ Other: _____

YOUR PARENTS:
☐ Have professed faith in Jesus Christ.
☐ Belong to a church, but seldom attend.
☐ Belong to a church, and attend faithfully.
☐ Don't discuss their beliefs with you.
☐ Other: _____

WHY DID YOU BECOME A CHRISTIAN?
☐ Influenced by family member(s).
☐ Influenced by friends.
☐ Influenced by respected person (teacher, etc.).
☐ Through preaching or reading Christian literature.
☐ God revealed His presence to me personally.
☐ Other: _____

HAVE YOU EVER BEEN BAPTIZED? _____ WHEN? _____

If so, describe the method (immersed, sprinkled)
of baptism: _____

HOW WOULD YOU DESCRIBE YOUR CONVERSION EXPERIENCE?
- ☐ Dramatic.
- ☐ Quiet.
- ☐ Vague.
- ☐ Uncertain.
- ☐ Other: _____

IF YOU ARE WORKING, HOW LONG HAVE YOU BEEN WORKING?
_____ years _____ months

IN THAT TIME, HOW MANY JOBS HAVE YOU HAD? _____

HAVE YOU FOLLOWED ANY RELIGIOUS GROUPS IN THE PAST? WHICH ONE(S)?
_____
_____

WRITE DOWN YOUR PAST RELIGIOUS OR SUPERNATURAL EXPERIENCES:
_____
_____

LIST TWO OR THREE PEOPLE WHO HAVE SIGNIFICANTLY
INFLUENCED YOUR LIFE:
1. _____
2. _____
3. _____

HOW DO YOU SHARE YOUR FAITH WITH OTHERS?
- ☐ Naturally, with freedom.
- ☐ With hesitation.
- ☐ Don't share with others.
- ☐ Out of a guilty compulsion.
- ☐ Don't know how.
- ☐ Other: _____

Previous Church Experience

Check [✓] each statement that is true for you:

WHAT KIND OF CHURCHES YOU HAVE ATTENDED IN THE PAST?
☐ I never attended a church before this one.
☐ Very formal churches.
☐ Catholic churches.
☐ Denominational churches.
    What kind: _____
☐ Charismatic churches.
☐ Other: _____

YOUR EXPERIENCE IN PREVIOUS CHURCHES HAS BEEN:
☐ Positive and encouraging.
☐ Mixed, some negative, some positive.
☐ Negative and discouraging.
☐ Neutral.
☐ List others below:

_____
_____
_____

WHAT HAS BEEN YOUR PREVIOUS ATTENDANCE IN CHURCH LIFE?
☐ Sunday worship: ☐ Regular   ☐ Irregular
☐ Sunday school: ☐ Regular   ☐ Irregular
☐ List or explain others below:

_____
_____
_____
_____

WHAT ARE THE THREE MOST UNFORGETTABLE BLESSINGS OR LESSONS YOU HAVE RECEIVED FROM GOD IN YOUR LIFE?
1. _____
2. _____
3. _____

Bible Knowledge Quiz

Instructions: Write the numbers of items in Column 2 which properly relate to items in Column 1.

____ The four Gospels

____ Paul

____ Emmanuel

____ Joseph

____ Peter

____ Ten Commandments

____ Turning Water Into Wine

____ Revelation

____ Judas

____ Bethlehem

____ Twelve

____ Blood of Jesus

____ David

____ Samson

1. First miracle of Jesus.

2. Last book of the Bible.

3. Birthplace of Jesus.

4. Number of Jesus' disciples.

5. Cleanses our sins.

6. Man of great strength.

7. Defeated Goliath.

8. Mary's husband.

9. Denied Jesus three times.

10. Law given to Moses.

11. Records the life of Jesus.

12. Writer of 13 books of the Bible.

13. Betrayed Jesus.

14. A name of Jesus.

Check your answers — See bottom of page 14.

How Would You Characterize Your Life?

Check [✓] each statement that is true for you:

HOW DO YOU VIEW YOUR LIFE BEFORE COMING TO CHRIST? WITH:
- ☐ Greatfulness and Contentment. ☐ Regret and Shame.
- ☐ Fear that the past will always haunt me.
- ☐ Recognition that God protected me and led me to Him.
- ☐ Other: _____

HOW DO YOU RELATE TO OTHER PEOPLE?
- ☐ Friendships come easy.   ☐ I often feel ignored by others.
- ☐ Friends are only around when things are going well.
- ☐ Friends are limited to work or official activities.
- ☐ Friends are rare, and I find myself alone a lot.
- ☐ Other: _____

HOW DO YOU RELATE TO YOUR PARENTS?
- ☐ I only relate to my father.   ☐ I only relate to my mother.
- ☐ We have a very strong relationship.
- ☐ We talk but we are not close.
- ☐ We do not relate to one another.
- ☐ Other: _____

SHARING ABOUT YOURSELF WITH OTHERS IS:
- ☐ Easy. I am generally transparent.
- ☐ A struggle. I share because it is good, but it does not come naturally.
- ☐ Fearful. I am scared that other people will not accept me.
- ☐ An unknown experience. I don't share who I am with others.
- ☐ Other: _____

HOW DO YOU VIEW MONEY?
- ☐ Making money has been the most important thing in my life.
- ☐ I have never had enough money to pay the bills.
- ☐ I always spend more than I make.
- ☐ I am content to live modestly on what I make.
- ☐ I find more joy in giving than in getting.
- ☐ Other: _____

SINCE BECOMING A CHRISTIAN, COMING TO CHURCH AND CELL GROUP IS:
☐ The best part of my week.
☐ Easy and exciting.
☐ A struggle, but I know it is good for me.
☐ Sporadic at best.
☐ Other: _____

SPENDING TIME WITH GOD AND TIME IN THE BIBLE IS:
☐ A powerful and fulfilling experience.
☐ Helpful in knowing how to live each day.
☐ Dull and hard.
☐ Not a regular experience.
☐ Other: _____

HOW DO YOU VIEW SERVING OTHERS?
☐ I enjoy serving others.
☐ I serve when someone asks me to.
☐ I don't like serving, but I do it anyway.
☐ I don't serve other people.
☐ Other: _____

HOW WOULD YOU DESCRIBE YOUR COMMITMENT LEVEL TO CHRIST?
☐ Jesus is everything to me.
☐ He is doing so much in my life that I love to tell others about Him.
☐ I know Jesus is real, but I can't seem to get my priorities straight.
☐ I struggle to do the right things, as I act in ways I should not.
☐ Sometimes, I don't want to be committed to Christ.
☐ Other: _____

WHAT DO YOU LIKE TO DO FOR FUN?
☐ Sports activities: _____
☐ Hobbies: _____
☐ Spend time with friends.
☐ Entertain people.
☐ Other: _____

How Do You Learn?

Check [✓] each statement that is true for you:

☐ I read a lot. Books are important to me when I want to learn.

☐ I learn by doing, by watching, and by being involved in things.

☐ I often listen to cassette tapes or CD's to help me learn.

☐ I like to find someone who knows what I want to know. I will get involved with such a person and develop skills.

☐ I don't have any special pattern for learning. It's not a strength in my life.

ACTIVITIES YOU ENJOY

(Rank your enjoyment level from 1 to 5, 5 being the highest.)

___ Helping other people with their problems.

___ Going to a party with lots of food and friends.

___ Working on a computer, or making something with my hands.

___ Playing competitive sports like tennis, etc.

___ Enjoying music or playing an instrument.

Did your preference not appear above? Write it below:

_____

Strongholds

Scripture talks about "strongholds" in our lives. These are areas where we seem to be constantly facing defeat, discouragement, or fear. We are often unable to move forward in our journey because of them.

Strongholds can defeat us spiritually. They rob us of our peace, love, and fellowship with God. Periods of intense stress often enlarge their power.

Are you struggling with areas in your life where you feel defeated? Few of us can wrestle with them alone. In the book of Acts, we find frequent examples of people being ministered to by others filled with the Holy Spirit.

Meeting with another person in your cell group can be a springboard to victory. Share your strongholds as you grow together.

Our Lord Jesus Christ is more powerful than any stronghold, and it is your birthright as God's child to be fully delivered from strongholds in your life.

On the next page are some strongholds common to many people. Prayerfully check [✓] each statement that is true or partially true for you. Later, you will be given the opportunity to share in private why you checked the statement.

- [ ] I had a poor relationship with my father/mother. Maybe that's why I find it hard to believe that God truly loves me.
- [ ] I have a hard time forgiving myself for things I've done in the past. I constantly dislike myself.
- [ ] I have been wrongly treated and hurt in the past. I find it hard to be set free of the inner anger I feel when remembering it.
- [ ] I have a sin or bad habit in my life that controls me. I try to change, but I really feel like a captive in this situation.
- [ ] I struggle with a sexual problem. I have never been able to break its control and the bad habits that go with it.
- [ ] I have trouble with addiction: overeating, gambling, exaggerating, smoking, drugs, alcohol, etc.
- [ ] I sometimes feel that my desire for money and possessions has a powerful control over me.
- [ ] I find it difficult to control my anger. It seems to well up from within me and to explode before I can stop it.
- [ ] I have a problem with anxiety. Sometimes I don't know why I am so anxious. I get anxious even about little things.
- [ ] I have many fears in my life. They include fears of loneliness, sickness, death, etc.
- [ ] I have contemplated suicide on several occasions.
- [ ] I have been involved in homosexuality.
- [ ] I find it hard to concentrate when I am reading the Bible and praying. It is as though a drowsiness comes on me.
- [ ] In the past, I have been involved in some occult practices (e.g., seances, witchcraft, etc.) or have been a member of a cult.
- [ ] I have been abused physically, mentally, or emotionally.
- [ ] I still have pornographic or sensual books/magazines in my home.
- [ ] I have had disappointing experiences with former churches.
- [ ] I hold up work as my most important activity. My life is consumed by my performance and achievement level.
- [ ] I find myself sleeping more than normal and have no desire to do anything productive.
- [ ] I have a great fear of speaking up or stating my opinion.
- [ ] I feel like I constantly have to be in a romantic relationship with a person of the opposite sex.
- [ ] _____

Cell Group Life is Important to You!

Many people believe that everything we learn must come from reading books or listening to lectures. Many church leaders today receive their primary training this way. The problem is that most of what we learn in life is caught, not taught. Most of us learn by observing others and then doing it ourselves. The disciples learned from Jesus this way.

Learning by watching others and imitating them is called modeling. Think of your own life. Have you ever listed the people you have used as a pattern for your own lifestyle? (These may be the same as on page 3.) Write the names of two people who have filled this special role for you below:

1. _____

2. _____

The art of relating to others is not learned from reading books. To learn how to relate to others, we must watch how others relate. Books can give us information about relationships, but we must observe people who are doing what the books talk about!

That is why every person needs parental models along with the models of brothers and sisters. These people give us our values. They set the atmosphere of the greater community. We need relationships with people with whom we can identify and whose actions we can copy.

The cell group is God's most practical design for this modeling to take place among Christians. In the urban world, people often don't understand what it is like to live responsibly with fellow believers. Perhaps your entry into your cell group will be the very first time in your life to experience true community.

We learn community by participating in it, not by just observing it. Learn to give love as well as receive it. Learn to be sensitive to others. For example, avoid dominating a cell discussion because this chokes off sharing by other cell members. Prepare yourself beforehand by listening to God so that you can build up others who need your affirmation.

Enter into the experience with all your heart! There will be more mature Christians you can select as good patterns for your own life. In time, you will become a model to those who are younger in Christ than you are.

"Would You Be My Mentor?"

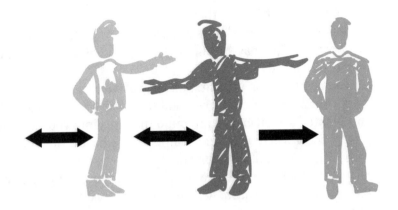

Every Christian in a cell group should become a part of a living chain of people who love and build up one another. Being helped, and being a helper — this is the New Testament pattern!

Perhaps you have felt you are a "second class Christian" because you don't know a lot of Scripture or because your prayer life is not strong. Nonsense! Martin Luther said, "The simplest peasant, armed with the Gospel, is mightier than a Pope!"

Your growth in Christ will depend on finding someone in your cell group who has taken three or four steps ahead of you, and who can show you where to place your feet next as you journey toward maturity. Discuss with your cell leader who that person might be. He or she will arrange for that person to be your "Mentor," if it is best for you both.

As you join hands with this person, there will be someone just a few steps behind you. Therefore, as you continue to grow, the time will soon come when your cell leader will ask you to hold this person's hand and be his or her guide. You will do with this person what your Mentor will have done with you. You do not need to worry that you won't know what to do, you have a Mentor who will teach you. If he does not know the answer, he himself has a Mentor who will be willing to help.

You'll keep in touch and meet regularly with the person you are mentoring. In special times of need, you may spend hours together, as good friends would do. Although your cell leader will always be ready to spend time with you, your main care-giver will be your Mentor. Your Mentor, the person you are mentoring, and you will create a special "triplet" for prayer and for sharing. You will be three links in a chain.

Having a Mentor and being a Mentor: that's what makes the cell group a vital gathering. Enter into this lifestyle with a total commitment to be God's person for others.

Your Journey Map

It is important for you to know that everyone in your cell group has a Journey Map. Each one is growing and is at a different stage of their spiritual journey. Your Journey Maps may be different, but you will all have a clear picture of the journey ahead.

Where are you right now on your first journey of your Christian growth? Honestly evaluate your present spiritual condition. For every question you are asked, your Mentor will enable you to build that area into your life. How wonderful it is to know where you are heading and to have a plan for your growth into a healthy and fulfilling individual!

Please remember that this is for your growth, so there is no reason to make up your response for someone else to see. This evaluation is for you alone, so be honest.

The following are the different marks that you must pass on your first journey as a new believer.

Dear Lord, please guide my mind as I evaluate my life. Help me to truly understand myself. I want to grow and glorify Your name. Amen.

(Rate the truthfulness of the following statements on a scale of 1 to 5, 5 being the highest.)

_____ **HAVING ASSURANCE OF MY SALVATION**
I understand what it means to be a Christian, and I have shared this with another person.

_____ **HAVING REGULAR DEVOTIONAL TIME**
I know how to have a devotional time, and I am taking steps to have one daily.

_____ **BAPTISM INTO THE BODY OF CHRIST**
I understand the meaning of baptism, and I am baptized into the Body of Christ.

_____ **BEING A PART OF THE FAMILY OF GOD**
I have a sense of being a part of a new family and understand that in this family, everyone must participate and contribute.

BEING AN ACTIVE MEMBER OF A CELL
I am an active member of a cell group and am discovering the roles that I can play in it.

REVISING MY VALUE SYSTEM
I understand that in the New Kingdom, there is a new value system. I am discerning personal values that are inappropriate in the Kingdom and I am adding others values that are needed to my lifestyle.

MEMORIZING THE SCRIPTURES
I understand the importance of hiding God's word in my heart, and I am memorizing Scripture.

SPENDING TIME IN PRAYER
I understand the importance of praying, and I am learning to listen to the voice of God.

ENGAGING IN SPIRITUAL WARFARE
I understand that Christians are engaging in spiritual warfare with the forces of evil, and I know how to resist the Devil.

BREAKING FREE OF STRONGHOLDS
I understand the concept of strongholds in a person's life, and I am breaking free of those that are in my own life.

BEING EMPOWERED BY THE HOLY SPIRIT
I understand and desire to be filled and empowered by the Holy Spirit, and I am learning to use the spiritual gifts.

BUILDING HEALTHY ATTITUDES
I realize the wrong attitudes in my life whether personal or social; I am taking steps to build healthy attitudes.

WITNESSING FOR JESUS
I realize that I need to share my new life with others, especially with those whom I relate to regularly. I have written out my testimony and know how to share it with others. I have testified to or have invited at least two people to come to cell group or celebration.

LINKING IN WITH A MENTOR
I understand the importance of having an older Christian to help me in my personal growth, and I am linked with a Mentor.

Your Journey Map

The following are the items of your Spiritual Journey as a New Believer. Check [✓] three items that you feel you need to have in the immediate future. Your evaluation in the last two pages and your present life situation can help you make the decision.

Linking with Mentor ☐

☐ Testifying Jesus

☐ Healthy Attitudes

☐ Power of Holy Spirit

Overcoming Strongholds ☐

☐ Spiritual Warfare

Time in Prayer ☐

☐ Memorizing Scriptures

Revising Value System ☐

☐ Active Cell Member

Part of God s Family ☐

Regular   ☐ Baptism
Devotional ☐

☐ Assurance of Salvation

How to Prepare Your Personal Testimony

Thoughtfully recall your conversion experience. Then write no more than two or three sentences describing it, using this outline taken from Paul's testimony in Acts 26:1-28:

MY LIFE BEFORE BECOMING A CHRISTIAN WAS LIKE THIS:

_____

_____

_____

_____

_____

THIS IS THE WAY I REALIZED THAT I NEEDED TO FOLLOW JESUS:

_____

_____

_____

_____

THESE ARE THE DETAILS OF HOW I ACTUALLY ACCEPTED CHRIST:

_____

_____

_____

_____

_____

THIS IS WHAT IT MEANS TO ME TO BE A CHRISTIAN:

_____

_____

_____

_____

_____

. . . CLOSE BY ASKING, HAS THIS EVER HAPPENED TO YOU?

Instructions for the Cell Leader

The Journey Guide for New Believers is designed to help you understand the spiritual, emotional, and intellectual background of your cell members. When you learn these things, you will be able to minister to them more effectively.

Give a copy of this booklet to all incoming cell members. Ask the new members to take it home and prayerfully complete each page. Explain that there are no right or wrong answers. The purpose of going through the booklet is to help pinpoint where they are in their spiritual journey and to help equip them for a fruitful life in Christ.

Schedule a time when you can meet and go through the completed *Journey Guide for New Believers* together. For this meeting, you will bring along the Mentor who will be a weekly support and encouragement for this person. If the Mentor cannot come, ask your intern to accompany you. Tell them that the meeting will only last about an hour and that you want to see where God has brought them so that you can better minister to them.

Begin with prayer. Then go through each page, explaining what each page means and asking if they have any questions. Ask the person to share what they checked off. *Tell them that they don't have to share anything that they are not ready to share.* You can also bring along a *Journey Guide* you have filled out in the past and share some of what you have checked off.

As you go through the pages, make a mental note of the areas of victory and the areas of special need. Do not write anything down during the meeting because this makes people uncomfortable. This is not a time to minister or pray for every need that arises as you move through the booklet. The point is to get to know your cell member, discover what God is doing in his or her life, and see what needs he or she might have. You might pray for one or two specific needs, but don't expect to meet every need in this meeting.

End your time together with prayer and encouragement. For some people they are taking a big risk in sharing their life with you. Encourage your new cell member by sharing how you see God moving in his or her life.